# Building Jerusalem

# Building Jerusalem

by
Michael Redhill

based on a concept and staged by
Ross Manson

Playwrights Canada Press
Toronto•Canada

**Playwrights Canada Press**
54 Wolseley Street, 2nd Floor
Toronto, Ontario  CANADA  M5T 1A5
(416) 703-0201    fax (416) 703-0059
info@puc.ca    http://www.puc.ca

**Playwrights Canada Press** acknowledges the support of
The Canada Council for the Arts for our publishing programme and
the Ontario Arts Council.

ONTARIO ARTS COUNCIL
CONSEIL DES ARTS DE L'ONTARIO

Cover photo of Stephan Beckon as Silas Rand by Dahlia Steinberg.
Cover by Elliott Smith.
Production Manager: Jodi Armstrong

**Canadian Cataloguing in Publication Data**

Redhill, Michael, 1966-
  Building Jerusalem

A play.
ISBN 0-88754-610-2

I. Title

PS8585.E3425B84  2001          C812'.54          C2001-930033-6
PR9199.3.R42B84  2001

First edition:  April 2001
Printed and bound by AGMV-Marquis at Quebec, Canada.

## PERFORMANCE HISTORY

**1996**: Initial workshop by Volcano as part of The Tarragon Spring Arts Fair, at the Tarragon Extra Space, Toronto, under the working title *In-door Amusements and Fireside Fun* (after Cassells' 1881 Book of parlour games etc.).

| | |
|---|---|
| **ALICE** | Sarah Chase |
| **ADELAIDE** | Claudia Moore |
| **AUGUSTA** | Leah Cherniak |
| **KARL** | Ross Manson |
| **SILAS** | Bill Coleman |

Music by Bill Brennan
Choreography by Claudia Moore
Initial script work by Ross Manson and Linda Griffiths
Conceived, Directed and Designed by Ross Manson

**1997**: Public Workshop of the newly titled *Building Jerusalem*, produced by Volcano in association with the Theatre Centre in Toronto: five showings of a work-in-progress.

| | |
|---|---|
| **ALICE** | Sarah Chase |
| **ADELAIDE** | Claudia Moore |
| **AUGUSTA** | Kim Renders |
| **KARL** | Ross Manson |
| **SILAS** | Stephan Beckon |

Text by Michael Redhill
Directed by Ross Manson
Choreography by Claudia Moore
Music by Bill Brennan
Dramaturgy by Ross Manson and Linda Griffiths
Set and Costumes Designed by Teresa Przybylski
Lighting Designed by Bonnie Beecher
Stage Managed by Erica Heyland and Kim Boyd
Production Management by Mark Ryder
Produced by Ross Manson

**1998**: A work-in-progress showing of Volcano's *Building Jerusalem* at the Damn Straight studio in Toronto.

| | |
|---|---|
| **ALICE** | Waneta Storms |
| **ADELAIDE** | Claudia Moore |
| **AUGUSTA** | Kim Renders |
| **KARL** | Ross Manson |
| **SILAS** | Stephan Beckon |

Text by Michael Redhill
Directed by Ross Manson
Choreography by Claudia Moore
Music by Bill Brennan
Dramaturgy by Ross Manson and Linda Griffiths
Set and Costumes Designed by Teresa Przybylski
Lighting Designed by Karen Bayer
Stage Managed by Erica Heyland and Shauna Janssen
Production Managed by John Kelly Cuthbertson
Produced by Ross Manson

**1999**: 2 work-in-progress showings of Volcano's *Building Jerusalem*, presented by Eastern Front's On the Waterfront festival in Halifax, Nova Scotia.

| | |
|---|---|
| **ALICE** | Sarah Chase |
| **ADELAIDE** | Claudia Moore |
| **AUGUSTA** | Kim Renders |
| **KARL** | Ross Manson |
| **SILAS** | Martin Julien |

Text by Michael Redhill
Directed by Ross Manson
Choreography by Claudia Moore
Music by Bill Brennan
Associate Director: Mark Christmann
Dramaturgy by Ross Manson and Linda Griffiths
Set and Costumes Designed by Teresa Przybylski
Lighting Designed by JP Robichaud
Stage Managed by JP Robichaud and Jennie Sinclair
Magic Consultant: Mike Segal
Production Management by David James
Produced by Camilla Holland and Ross Manson

*Building Jerusalem* was developed and produced by Volcano, and premiered at the Factory Theatre, Toronto, in January 2000 with the following cast:

| | |
|---|---|
| **ALICE** | Sarah Chase |
| **ADELAIDE** | Claudia Moore |
| **AUGUSTA** | Kim Renders |
| **KARL** | Ross Manson |
| **SILAS** | Martin Julien |

Written by Michael Redhill, based on an idea by Ross Manson
Directed by Ross Manson
Associate Director Mark Christmann
Dramaturgy by Linda Griffiths and Ross Manson
Choreography by Claudia Moore
Music by Bill Brennan
Set designed by Teresa Przybylski
Costumes designed by Michelle Smith
Lighting designed by JP Robichaud
Stage Management by Erica Heyland and Jennie Sinclair
Production Management by Michelle Ramsey
Alternate Pianist: David Restivo
Crew: Stephanie Tjelios, Anna-Marie Braet, Terri Park and Chris Prideaux
Photography: John Lauener
Graphic Design: Elliott Smith
Publicity: Sally Szuster
Produced by Camilla Holland and Ross Manson, in association with the Factory Theatre

"The best new play thus far in the 21st century... NNNN" —*NOW Magazine*
"[a] delightful play... whimsical and intelligent" —*The Globe & Mail*
"a sparkling fusion of drama, music and dance... delightful"
—*The Toronto Star*
"delightfully entertaining and highly thought provoking..."
—*The Toronto Sun*
"uniformly excellent... bright, exhilarating" —*eye weekly*

Winner of Toronto's Dora awards for Best Play and Best Production
Nominated for 7 Dora awards: Best Play (Michael Redhill), Best Production (Volcano), Best Director (Ross Manson), Best Actor (Martin Julien), Best Actress (Kim Renders), Best Set Design (Teresa Przybylski), Best Costume Design (Michelle Smith).

## CHARACTERS

| | |
|---|---|
| **ALICE** | a young woman, 21 |
| **ADELAIDE** Hoodless | a domestic scientist from Hamilton, 42 |
| **AUGUSTA** Stowe-Gullen | a doctor, from Toronto, 42 |
| **KARL** Pearson | a scientist, from London, England, 42 |
| **SILAS** Tertius Rand | a missionary, from Nova Scotia, 42 |

Note: Of the five, only Alice is fictional, and only Silas Rand wasn't actually 42 in 1899.

## BACKGROUND INFORMATION ON THE CHARACTERS

*Building Jerusalem* gathers together on New Year' Eve, 1899, in Toronto, a group of Victorian characters—four Canadians and an Englishman. Of the five, four actually existed. They are:

**Adelaide Hoodless:** A resident of Hamilton, Ontario; instrumental in the founding of the YWCA and the Victorian Order of Nurses in Canada. Adelaide Hoodless was a pioneer in developing the study of "Domestic Science" for Canadian girls, and founded the first Institute for the Study of Domestic Science in Canada. She was an avid conference-goer and well connected. This allowed her the chance, while attending an International Women's Council meeting in London, to shake the hand of Queen Victoria. She was firmly against women's suffrage, or the notion of women being allowed to enter the professions. She believed strongly in a better education for women as mothers, wives, and nurses, and was a staunch advocate of family life and the division of labour therein.

**Karl Pearson:** A resident of London, England; fellow of the Royal Society; a brilliant Darwinist, physicist and mathematician. Karl Pearson helped develop the science of biometrical statistics, was the first to offer mathematical proof of the theory of natural selection, and anticipated aspects of the theory of relativity. He was ambitious and productive—he taught, wrote many books on a wide range of subjects, and founded a respectable scientific journal which is published to this day. He was also an avowed racist, and was one of the pioneers of the science of eugenics—which concerned itself, among other things, with the selective breeding of humans in order to improve the race. This science was to become very popular and generally considered very progressive in the Victorian era. Karl Pearson was also an ardent Germanophile, as evidenced by the self-chosen spelling of his first name.

**Silas Tertius Rand:** A resident of rural Nova Scotia, the son of a bricklayer, and a Baptist missionary, Silas Rand devoted his life to Protestant missionary work among the Mi'kmaq of Nova Scotia and New Brunswick. He translated the bible into Micmac, developed the first Mi'kmaq/English dictionary, and is the primary translator of Mi'kmaq legends into written English. He believed in integrated education, and in rights of citizenship for aboriginal peoples, yet still believed them to be "semi-savages" that it was his task to convert to Christianity. He was primarily a self-taught linguist who could speak nearly twenty languages. Silas Rand left the Baptist church later in his life, considering it too corrupt, and threw himself on the mercy of God in order to survive. He lived in this fashion until the age of eighty.

**Augusta Stowe-Gullen:** A resident of Toronto, Ontario; the first woman in Canada to graduate from a Canadian medical school; and the daughter of Emily Stowe, Canada's first woman doctor. Augusta Stowe-Gullen had a private practice—shared with her husband—on Spadina Avenue in Toronto and delivered the first baby at the new Women's College Hospital in that city. In her later life, she was one of the suffragists most instrumental in securing the vote for Canadian women, and was a strong believer in the right of any woman to have the freedom to choose the direction her life was to take. She received the Order of the British Empire for her work.

To these four is added a fictional character named **Alice**. Alice is a woman about to turn twenty-one and was inspired by Alice in Wonderland, and the mythical figure of Truth—the daughter of Time. Who she really might be, though, is of course up to the audience.

## SETTING

The Grange House in Toronto. It is New Year's Eve, 1899.

## A NOTE ON STYLE

The scenes should move swiftly from one to another. Except where indicated, there are no blackouts. Alice is the only character who is able to relate directly to the audience.

## A NOTE ON THE MUSIC

The lyrics reproduced in this play are in the public domain. The music itself has not been included here, but can be found at a major library, or by inquiring through Playwrights Union of Canada (address on copyright page).

## ALICE

*A proscenium stage covered by a large blue silk
curtain. A clock chimes. Behind the curtain, lights
come up on ALICE, a glowing figure. She sings.*

ALICE    There was a wee wifey rolled up in a blanket,
Nineteen times as high as the moon.
And what she did there, I canna declare,
But under her arm she carried the sun.

*The silk falls to reveal ALICE. She is a sparkling
young woman dressed in the style of the late
1800s.*

Wee wifey, wee wifey, wee wifey, said I,
Oh what are you doing up there so high?
I'm blowing the cold clouds out of the sky.
Well done, well done, wee wifey, said I.

*The silk disappears. A few notes of "Auld Lang
Syne" are heard. The clock finishes chiming.*

## OUR STORY

ALICE    When our story begins, it is a cold, dark New Year's
Eve, and the windows are white with frost. (*happy
with the sound of that*) Yes. The revellers are off to
their parties, there's a quiet clip-clop in the distance
under the gas lamps and the snow-covered trees.
Soon enough, the bells at City Hall will bring in the
new century, and here, at the Grange, the illustrious
guests of the famous and wealthy Goldwin Smith
will raise their glasses... (*she pauses to consider this*)
er, no, no, that's not right. You see, the bells *will*
chime, but poor Mr. Smith will *still* be stuck in a
dreadful blizzard, while I take the carefully chosen
guests, who all think they're here to, nooo, that's
not it either. How about: Goldwin Smith's *niece*, yes,
his callow but genuinely lovely young *niece*,
pressed into duty by the turn of events, or rather by
the turn of the new – *Oh Piddle!* Sometimes it is so
very difficult to know where to start! (*We hear a few*

*more notes of "Auld Lang Syne." ALICE is struck by an idea.*) That's it: our story begins when a mysterious young girl offers her hand, (*As she describes the following actions, she does them. This is her first magic trick of the evening.*) which is then covered with a beautiful blue handkerchief, while her other hand begins to conjure... (*She whips the silk away to reveal a bowl of raspberries.*) Raspberries? Goodness, I wonder what these are for? (*The doorbell rings.*) That did it! How clever of me!

## SNOW

*All enter, already in conversation, a jolly-sounding gathering. KARL has just told a joke, and everyone is laughing, at least politely. ALICE is standing apart watching in wonder.*

*The four guests are keen, for their own reasons, to be here. They are a capable group, and each will look upon the other's rudeness—when it comes— more with amusement or fascination than anger or hurt. The exception in all of this is SILAS, who has a somewhat different agenda.*

**AUGUSTA**    Very funny, Dr. Pearson.

**ADELAIDE**   (*quoting the punchline*) If only they could do the same thing for corsets! Honestly, Dr. Pearson, you're quite a panic!

**KARL**       Well, it *is* a remarkable invention, the wireless.

               *ADELAIDE dissolves in laughter once more.*

**AUGUSTA**    No more so than the corset, itself. And both invented by men, I'd dare say.

**SILAS**      Miss?

**ALICE**      (*stirred out of wonderment*) Yes?

**SILAS**      Goldwin Smith, our host, he *will* be here shortly.

| | |
|---|---|
| **ALICE** | Oh yes! |
| **SILAS** | How shortly? |
| **ALICE** | Well, the snow. |
| **KARL** | The snow. |
| **ADELAIDE** | What snow. |
| **ALICE** | (*gesturing beyond them*) There's a terrible blizzard, Mrs. Hoodless. |

> *They all turn to look. They see a storm raging and snow that wasn't there only minutes ago when they arrived.*

| | |
|---|---|
| **ADELAIDE** | Goodness. |
| **KARL** | Where on earth did that come from. |
| **AUGUSTA** | It's quite beautiful. |
| **ADELAIDE** | Yes, it is. |
| **KARL** | Only in the Alps, ladies. In the colonies, snow is simply an impediment to one's progress out of the colonies. |
| **AUGUSTA** | (*smiling*) And Heaven forfend we should impede that. |
| **ADELAIDE** | You know, Dr. Pearson, we're not actually a colony anymore. Not for thirty-two years now. |
| **KARL** | Really. Good for you. (*to ALICE*) Miss, I think I shall have a hot toddy to ease the wait for our snowbound host. Anyone else? |
| **ALICE** | I'm sorry, Dr. Pearson, Uncle prefers that alcohol not– |
| **KARL** | Uncle? (*realizing she isn't a maid*) Oh! I'm sorry, I thought you were– |

ALICE      No, I'm not. I'm actually–

KARL      (*His interest is now piqued.*) His niece–

ALICE      Yes–

KARL      Charming–

ALICE      And there are no hot toddies.

KARL      Pity. Some of your *Uncle's* best brandy, then. (*He sees from the look on her face that there is no alcohol of any kind.*) What, no brandy either?

ALICE      Would you like a raspberry?

KARL      Is it fermented?

AUGUSTA      (*enjoying herself*) Reverend Rand, excuse me, but did I hear correctly? That you're visiting from Nova Scotia?

SILAS      (*curtly*) Yes, Dr. Stowe-Gullen. You heard correctly.

ADELAIDE      Heavens, Nova Scotia! How did you find the train out to Toronto?

SILAS      I busied myself with some reading. The forty-seven hours went quickly.

KARL      That must have been some book.

SILAS      The Bible? Yes, Dr. Pearson, it is "some book."

AUGUSTA      And so you've come all this way for a New Year's Eve party?

SILAS      No, Madam. My train back is to leave in two-and-a-half hours. I only accepted Mr. Smith's offer to bring me to Toronto to see my brother, who was on his deathbed.

ADELAIDE      I'm very, very sorry.

| | |
|---|---|
| **AUGUSTA** | And Goldwin Smith paid your passage? |
| **SILAS** | Yes. |
| **ALICE** | Why do you ask, Dr. Stowe-Gullen? |
| **AUGUSTA** | Only that Mr. Smith's generosity comes as rather a surprise. Just as being invited to the Grange at all came as rather a surprise. (*explaining*) The man is not known to be a friend of women with careers. |
| **ADELAIDE** | Then why come, Auggie? But you know, I, for one, am very interested in meeting this Mr. Goldwin Smith. |
| **AUGUSTA** | I'm sure you are, "Addie." And when you go to shake hands, will your palm be facing sideways, or up? |

*ADELAIDE smiles showing her teeth. Beat.*

| | |
|---|---|
| **KARL** | Well, the man made it clear he wants to see *me*. You know, he actually cabled me in the middle of my lecture tour— (*to ALICE*) Pearson's Statistical Proof of Natural Selection—and he said I absolutely must come to discuss some publishing– |
| **SILAS** | Excuse me, Miss... |
| **KARL** | –ideas. |
| **ALICE** | It's Alice. |
| **SILAS** | Please give my regards to Mr. Smith. I should have liked to thank him in person for his charity to me. But I must leave now if I am to reach the station on time. |
| **ALICE** | Oh, but Reverend, there will be no trains tonight. Not with all this snow. But I'm sure Uncle will be here soon, and in the meantime, we can relax and enjoy the delightful company we find ourselves in. |

*A few glances are exchanged.*

ADELAIDE     Excuse me, but Reverend Rand, surely you were
             not planning to usher in the new century whilst on
             a train?

SILAS        I thought it fitting to leave Sodom under cover of
             darkness.

             *Pause.*

KARL         Well, at least in Sodom, there was something to do
             of an evening.

## HOT BUTTER

             *An odd light. ALICE looks at each of them as they
             speak their lines out.*

SILAS        I try whenever possible, not to look at my own
             penis. Even when I am bathing.

AUGUSTA      I have an irresistible urge, when examining
             newborns, to pop their feet into my mouth and
             suck on them.

KARL         I think it refreshing to occasionally have one's
             buttocks vigorously pummelled.

ADELAIDE     I am inordinately fond of butter.

             *Light change. They are back in the parlour. The
             group is slightly affected by this shift.*

AUGUSTA      I beg your pardon?

ADELAIDE     I like butter.

ALICE        Oh wonderful! Well then, would anyone care for
             tea?

             *Blackout. Music.*

## HUNGER

> *Lights up. A mirror appears at the top of the scene. AUGUSTA will glance in it briefly. For the next four scenes, the guests are wandering the halls, each with a cup of tea.*

**AUGUSTA**   Blast it... I thought this would take an hour at most. And now our host is God-forsaken in a howling snow storm, and I'm stuck here at loose ends with amateur hospitality. And who is this young girl? (*AUGUSTA is intrigued – ALICE, also holding a cup of tea, appears in the mirror behind her.*) I've never heard of Goldwin Smith having a niece – not that *I'd* know, of course. Well, he's welcome to her – she reminds me of Jane Austen's Emma, that precocious... (*She freezes.*)

**ALICE**   (*stepping through the mirror*) ...I don't think so! Emma was a meddler! I'm not a meddler. I'm not. I remind you of your friend Mary, from England–

**AUGUSTA**   (*unfreezes, slightly confused*) ...of my friend Mary. From England.

**ALICE**   Goodness, Dr. Stowe-Gullen, I've read about her. She is the one in prison. Do you really know her?

**AUGUSTA**   Yes. Very well. Through the Women's Council. We met in Chicago.

**ALICE**   The papers say she keeps trying to kill herself.

**AUGUSTA**   It's called a hunger strike.

**ALICE**   A hunger strike. So, she's starving herself because she wants to vote?

**AUGUSTA**   Yes. Except they won't let her. They won't let her vote and they won't let her die. So they force feed her.

**ALICE**   How can they make her eat if she doesn't want to?

| AUGUSTA | Alice.... Do you know what is happening now in New York and London in the women's suffrage movement? |
| ALICE | No, Dr. Stowe-Gullen, I confess I don't. I don't even know what's happening here. |
| AUGUSTA | Well. Let's get some more tea, then. |

## PURE SCIENCE

| KARL | And then, you see, a *pure* science is an act of mind. It is the cerebellum cracking the whip over the dray horse of theory. It is the synapse dropping seed into the furrow of idea. It is Tycho Brahe insisting that stars exist beyond the moon's orbit. It is Darwin riding off on his turtle. (*He chuckles.*) |
| ALICE | But didn't Tycho Brahe also think the sun revolved around the earth? |
| KARL | Well.... Yes he did. But such was the ignorance of his time. |
| ALICE | Oh. But Darwin is still right, isn't he? |
| KARL | Well, of course Darwin is right. I say, that's an odd way to– |
| ALICE | So far... he's still right. |

## INFUSION

| SILAS | It's like making tea, Miss Alice: a silver ball full of crisp, rich pekoe leaves is immersed in hot water. Immediately, around the ball, tendrils of dark pigment begin to seep out and mix into the water, like smoke which twists against a pure blue sky. Involutions of colour which spiral to a single hue. |
| ALICE | I see. |

SILAS        Now, imagine: your body is that teacup, and the water within is your soul. And the round silver ball carries your first thought of God. That is the nature of faith: an irreversible infusion.

ALICE        Irreversible.

SILAS        Yes.

ALICE        Like Darwin riding off on his turtle.

SILAS        I beg your pardon?

## THE AGE TO MARRY

ADELAIDE        Alice, dear, now that we are friends... I've wanted... well, I notice something a little distracted about you.

ALICE        Oh, I'm sorry, it's just – having you all here – a doctor, a scientist, a missionary, and you with your new domestic science institute – all so accomplished. And here I am, about to turn twenty-one, and I've no thought in my head about what I should do with my life, and no one to tell me. I don't even have a suitor!

ADELAIDE        Aha! So that's it! Alice, dear, many women find their soulmates at a later age. I have a cousin who married at twenty-three, and all is well in her world I can tell you. Seven children and she's still under thirty.

ALICE        Thank you Mrs. Hoodless. It's nice to know there's hope.

ADELAIDE        Listen, dear. Don't despair of your future. You are an angel. Besides, a girl is not truly old until twenty-five.

       *Beat.*

ALICE        Did you call me an angel, Mrs. Hoodless?

**ADELAIDE**   You are. You're the picture of innocence and a remarkable young girl. Hosting a party of strangers like this with hardly anything but your wits to keep their attention.

**ALICE**   You must all be terribly bored. I am thinking perhaps playing a game or two might pass the time more amiably, until Uncle arrives.

**ADELAIDE**   What an excellent idea!

**ALICE**   A party isn't a party without games, is it?

**ADELAIDE**   You'd be surprised how many people don't understand that.

> *A rousing excerpt of the "Wee Wifey" refrain, then immediately to:*

### A GAME: DONKEY DO

> *The players are seated. Each player has invented a gesture for themselves which takes up two beats, and resembles something a donkey might do. All players have also learned all the other players' gestures. A four/four rhythm is established with the feet or hands. To this rhythm the words, "I am a donkey, this is what the donkeys do" are chant- ed. Immediately after the word "do," the person who is "it" begins by doing their own gesture for two beats and then someone else's gesture for two beats. This passes the "ball" to the person whose gesture was just done. Without missing a beat, this second person must repeat their own gesture, and then choose someone else's donkey to do. The speed of the game increases until someone stumbles and earns a forfeit. It is an absolutely ridiculous spectacle.*

> *All play. KARL has chosen a rude gesture meant to provoke SILAS and consistently passes the "ball" to the minister whenever he has the chance. As they play:*

ALICE      (*to the audience*) In the game of Donkey Do, a group of people imagines that they are donkeys, and must do as donkeys do on cue. It's a demanding game. And everyone is obliged to learn what everyone else's donkey does, or they forfeit the right to play. You are also eliminated if you don't pay attention, if you're clumsy, or if you begin to think too much.

KARL      (*responding to SILAS' stoppage*) Aha!

SILAS      No. (*referring to KARL's donkey*) I don't think a donkey would do that.

AUGUSTA      But Reverend, I thought we were all being perfect asses.

KARL      Miss Alice, might we have a ruling?

ALICE      I'm afraid donkeys aren't allowed opinions, Reverend. You have earned a forfeit. Go dance in the corner!

> *Music. SILAS goes to the corner and performs an elaborate Can Can.*

## BABEL

*The group is seated in the parlour.*

ADELAIDE      But what are you doing living in the wilds of Nova Scotia among such frightful savages?

SILAS      They are being brought over to Christ. We've been translating the bible, you know, into Mi'kmaq. (*He pronounces it mig-maw.*)

KARL      I'm sorry? Mig-what?

SILAS      We call them "Micmac" in English.

AUGUSTA      So, you *speak* Micmac.

SILAS      I do.

ALICE      Well isn't that tricky. Three languages.

KARL      I speak three myself. German's my favourite. Do you know any German?

SILAS      Ah, yes I do. German's a fine language.

ALICE      So, *four*.

SILAS      Actually – twelve.

KARL      Twelve.

SILAS      I am a bit of a sponge for other vocabularies. I'm afraid I can speak and write English, French, Micmac, Latin, Greek—modern and ancient— Hebrew, Italian, German, Spanish, Maliseet and Mohawk. But Micmac is my favourite. (*Pause.*) You can't know the anguish of being among such an innocent and beautiful peoples as the Micmac and know that they are going to burn in Hell.

AUGUSTA      Burn in *Hell*.

SILAS      They have been taught to preserve their barbaric ways, even when they've been given the chance to become like white men. Thank God this is finally changing.

ALICE      Do you know any of their stories?

SILAS      Oh yes.

ALICE      I love stories! What are they about?

SILAS      Hunting, great battles. Magic.

ALICE      Magic? Tell us.

SILAS      I don't think.

ADELAIDE      Please...

SILAS   Well... there's the old woman, Noogoomich, chipping a piece of beaver bone into a pot. But when her guests arrive, the pot is full to the brim with moose meat.

KARL   Oh goodie, moose meat.

SILAS   (*beat*) But my favourite is the story of the three kings. You see, a family is starving to death, and their last hope is that three wise kings in a faraway land will save them. So, one of the sons journeys through a wilderness full of terrible trials seeking the court of these legendary kings. After what seems like months, he finds it, they receive him, give him seven blessings and magical seed for his family. Suddenly, he finds himself at home again. The magic seeds are planted and... in any case, he saves his family... (*He pauses, suddenly troubled.*)

ADELAIDE   Please, go on.

SILAS   He saves them from certain death. But just before the harvest, the boy's father has a dream. He senses the crop is in great danger, from some terrible evil, so he goes out to the fields to pray. When, after two days, he does not return, the boy goes to seek his father, and to join him in prayer. The weather stays good, the crop grows tall, yet the men do not return. Finally, several weeks later, at harvest time, when the women are reaping the wheat, they find them. The son holding his father, their mouths open to the skies. Dead.

    *Pause.*

KARL   That's it?

SILAS   That is the story of the three kings.

ADELAIDE   Whatever does it mean?

SILAS   Well– (*He clears his throat.*) –clearly, it is both the story of Moses leading his people to the promised land, and of Christ's journey through the wilderness.

KARL        What.

SILAS       Somehow, the truths of the bible find their way into
            these legends. And now, we are entrusted with
            retranslating these gospels back into their original
            forms and returning the word of truth,
            unadulterated, to them.

KARL        My God. How is it the story of Moses. Or of Christ?

SILAS       It's obvious. (*gaining momentum*) A people, not
            unlike the Jews, are enslaved – but in this case to
            hunger. Someone interposes for them and that is
            Moses. The walk to the kings is Christ in the
            wilderness, the three kings are the Trinity, the seeds
            are the ten commandments, and then both the
            father and the son die, one as Moses before Israel,
            the other as Christ, for the sins of his people.

KARL        What absolute miscegenation! You've shoe-horned
            every possible permutation of your own myths into
            the Micmac's to make theirs sound like bargain-rate
            bible stories.

SILAS       Well, they are obviously rooted–

KARL        I think not. I think you are working too hard to
            prove these people are *like* us. They're not. And
            their stories prove it. Reverend, people are separate
            for a reason. It's sustaining; it's right and just. If
            God wanted us among the Micmac, why did he not
            plant us on the same soil as them?

ALICE       (*gleefully erupting*) Oh, this is good!

KARL        It is?

ALICE       Excellent.

## OF SUITS AND SILK

*Another room in the house.*

**KARL**  Well, that was amusing. I love a good campfire tale. Do you suppose he wears a loin-cloth under that ridiculous suit of his?

**AUGUSTA**  Why do you suppose I would be speculating as to the Reverend's underclothing, Dr. Pearson?

**KARL**  I do not suspect you of prurience, Madam. I am simply passing the friendly time of day with a colleague.

**AUGUSTA**  Oh – am I a colleague?

**KARL**  Unless you think I'd be handy with holy water or a pair of knitting needles, yes, I think we are the only two here with something in common.

**AUGUSTA**  And what would that be?

**KARL**  Science, breeding, and exceptional taste in clothing.

**AUGUSTA**  Ah! You like my dress – I'm flattered.

**KARL**  I can always spot good cloth—fine beads but nothing showy—pillars of female society stuff.

**AUGUSTA**  Oh, Dr. Pearson. I admire the swiftness with which you can label a specimen.

**KARL**  My eye is trained, Madam. (*He takes out a cigar case.*)

**AUGUSTA**  Are those rum-tipped, by any chance?

**KARL**  Why yes, they are. Would you care for one?

**AUGUSTA**  Thank you.

**KARL**  (*pleasantly surprised*) Really ?

**AUGUSTA**  Not what you'd expect from a pillar of female society? Never judge a book by its cover, Dr. Pearson.

| | |
|---|---|
| **KARL** | You're quite right. (*He lights her cigar.*) I must get under the covers more often. |
| **AUGUSTA** | Hence your sudden interest in the Reverend's undergarments? |
| **KARL** | (*laughing*) Madam! Your banter would be at home in my club. But honestly, do you not think this Reverend Rand is mad? |
| **AUGUSTA** | So missionary work is madness by you? |
| **KARL** | Or rubbish. For God's sake, the Micmacs don't need the Bible, they need the isolation they have always had. What that man is doing will only lead to disaster. |
| **AUGUSTA** | You think so? |
| **KARL** | Don't you? Granted, it is wise to prepare the way, so the foreign peoples are ready when you arrive. But to run the shops, my dear Dr. Stowe-Gullen. Not to act like masters of the house. And if you treat an *abo* the same way you treat Lord Carnarvon, your world will just disintegrate. |
| **AUGUSTA** | And Heaven knows where we would find quality clothing then. |
| **KARL** | Mockery, no less – that is an arrow in my heart. |
| **AUGUSTA** | Goodness. Such excellent aim and such a small target. (*She exits.*) |
| **KARL** | Well. What delightful company one finds in Toronto. (*He looks at his watch.*) Oh God. Where *is* this damned Goldwin Smith! |

*The others enter abruptly.*

| | |
|---|---|
| **SILAS** | Language. |
| **KARL** | (*about to start an argument with SILAS*) Language?! |
| **ALICE** | Wait! I want a baby elephant! Go! |

## GAME: BABY ELEPHANT

*Music. They use various items of clothing to transform KARL and SILAS into an elephant. A frenetic dance. Freeze.*

ALICE      (*admiring her handiwork*) There. I think that's perfect. (*She takes AUGUSTA's hand.*) Come. Follow the leader.

## THE SHRINKING UNIVERSE

*ALICE and AUGUSTA are playing follow the leader.*

ALICE      I hardly remember my childhood – it seems so long ago.

AUGUSTA      Mine was full of instruction. My mother was a doctor.

ALICE      Yes I know, everyone has heard of Emily Stowe.

AUGUSTA      You must have had some time to play though, didn't you Alice?

ALICE      Oh yes. I still make time now.

AUGUSTA      And what do you do?

ALICE      I play with imaginary friends. (*She points at an imaginary chasm.*) Jump. Don't you make time to play?

AUGUSTA      Perhaps I should.

ALICE      You don't really mean that do you?

AUGUSTA      Oh, Alice. When I was little, I used to sneak out into our backyard, lie on a blanket—so as not to dirty my nightdress—and look up at all the stars. I had been taught in school that the universe was infinite; and so I would try to imagine what infinity was.

**ALICE**     Well that's a wonderful game!

**AUGUSTA**   Yes, it was... for a while. But I stopped playing it.

**ALICE**     Why?

**AUGUSTA**   Because my imagination just wasn't big enough
              to take on the whole universe. So I settled for
              something smaller, Alice. Smaller, busier, and with
              just enough curiosity left over to wonder who
              might be at the board meeting on Thursday, and
              what they might say about me this time. Oh, what
              we adults get up to.... It's all a bit repetitive.

**ALICE**     And that isn't fun?

**AUGUSTA**   No, Alice. It isn't fun.

### MUMMY

*A strange light. ALICE uses her silk to "conjure"
ADELAIDE in the guise of Emily Stowe.*

**ADELAIDE**  (*as Emily Stowe*) Are we comfy, Auggie?

**AUGUSTA**   Yes mummy.

**ADELAIDE**  What is my little girl going to be when she grows
              up?

**AUGUSTA**   A princess with a flowing dress.

**ADELAIDE**  What else?

**AUGUSTA**   A zookeeper!

**ADELAIDE**  (*getting impatient*) Yes... and?

**AUGUSTA**   (*sadly*) A doctor.

**ADELAIDE**  Like mummy! Good girl! Now, what is this? What
              do we call this, pumpkin?

AUGUSTA   Umm... zygomatic arch.

ADELAIDE   Good girl. And these?

AUGUSTA   Tragus... and antitragus.

ADELAIDE   And what is your nose made of?

AUGUSTA   Puppy dog tails.

ADELAIDE   *Augusta!*

AUGUSTA   Cartilage.

ADELAIDE   Good girl. (*She gives her a kiss.*) Mummy loves you.

AUGUSTA   I know Mummy.

*A clock chimes. ALICE vanishes.*

## CRYING BABY

ADELAIDE   Augusta?

AUGUSTA   Hm?

ADELAIDE   Augusta, are you alright?

AUGUSTA   Oh – Adelaide. Sorry, were you...?

ADELAIDE   I was asking if you heard a baby crying?

AUGUSTA   A baby? There are no babies here, Adelaide. It's just the clock chiming.

ADELAIDE   I thought I heard a baby crying. But it stopped. (*Pause.*) Goodness. Nine o'clock already – and no sign of anyone?

AUGUSTA   And only three hours till midnight. Oh dear. I never thought I'd spend this night—of all nights— marooned. Yet here we are. Stepping over the precipice with nothing but the scrutiny of strangers for comfort.

ADELAIDE   Augusta, that's a bit dire; whatever do you mean?

AUGUSTA   Oh nothing. It's just all these games I haven't played since I was a girl – and then hardly ever. I feel a little too "on display."

ADELAIDE   It will do the doctor good. And at least you don't keep losing, like our poor Reverend. (*They share a smile.*) You know, Auggie, you would make such a fine mother yourself. It's strange to me that you and John have no children.

## BRICKBATS

AUGUSTA   You think it's a waste.

ADELAIDE   No... I just. Well, you're a married woman, Augusta. There's nothing wrong with you, and people are beginning to...

AUGUSTA   It doesn't matter to me what people say.

ADELAIDE   You know, you'll get old, Augusta, and getting the vote won't seem so important. Having someone to visit on a Saturday afternoon, however... someone who will look after you.

AUGUSTA   Oh Addie. How can we be friends? You are a cave woman. If I hear on the wireless in forty years that it was the women's vote that ousted so-and-so from office – I won't care what I'm doing all of a Saturday afternoon. Anyway, I'll have John.

ADELAIDE   And you'll have me. You will. But when will you see that you are fighting the wrong fight? You can tell John right now who you think he should vote for. You can decide as a family how to cast your ballot.

AUGUSTA   Adelaide – why should a woman marry to have a voice? Why? And what of widows? Who do they pass their opinion on to – the postman? You *know* what you're saying is nonsense, but you just don't want to rock the boat.

**ADELAIDE**   I don't wish to get *in* the boat at all, Augusta.

**AUGUSTA**   Honestly, you're like talking to a post.

**ADELAIDE**   (*calling to ALICE*) Alice!

**ALICE**   (*appearing instantly*) Yes?

**ADELAIDE**   Alice, dear. Do you know in London, where women are agitating for the vote, that many have been known to daintily tie a string around a brick and then heave that brick through a window?

**ALICE**   A string?

**AUGUSTA**   The string is an ingenious way to retrieve one's brick, should the need arise again.

**ADELAIDE**   Perhaps when they are released from prison! And *that* is supposed to help the cause. That is supposed to make women "equal" to men. Violence!

**ALICE**   Are you two arguing?

**AUGUSTA**   Karl Pearson argues. We are pursuing a philosophical difference.

**ADELAIDE**   Alice, would *you* like to vote?

**ALICE**   On what?

**ADELAIDE**   In general.

**ALICE**   I don't know. Should I want to?

**AUGUSTA**   Goodness. Are the two of you related?

**ALICE**   I wouldn't want to break windows.

**ADELAIDE**   And why would you? There is no need to be violent to play your role in society.

**AUGUSTA**   No, you could always raise committees. And write polite manifestos.

**ADELAIDE**   Don't pish-tosh my manifestos, Augusta! If you sat on any committee that actually did real work, you would see progress. But no, you have chosen to be a barren suffragette.

**AUGUSTA**   Adelaide, really.

*There is a standoff between the two women. ALICE looks uncomfortably on. Finally, almost a question.*

**ALICE**   If I got the vote...

*The men enter to listen.*

**ALICE**   (*to AUGUSTA*) I'd use it. (*to ADELAIDE*) I think...

*The next two lines are spoken together.*

**ADELAIDE**   Alice, for Heaven's sake–

**AUGUSTA**   Alice, you can't just–

**ALICE**   (*quickly*) Wait! I want a Wee Wifey! Go!

### SONG: WEE WIFEY

*Sung in elaborate harmony by all five.*

**ALL**   There was a wee wifey rolled up in a blanket,
Nineteen times as high as the moon.
And what she did there, I canna declare,
But under her arm she carried the sun.

Wee wifey, wee wifey, wee wifey, said I,
Oh what are you doing up there so high?
I'm blowing the cold clouds out of the sky.
Well done, well done, wee wifey, said I.

*The four guests freeze.*

**ALICE**   (*sighs with satisfaction*) Ahh. Harmony. If only briefly...

## A GAME: ZULU

*The group is again seated in the parlour. They all play the game ALICE describes.*

ALICE    In the game of Zulu, a group of people play tag, but with eye contact. The person who is "it" can make someone else "it" simply by looking at them and saying "Zulu." The new "it" can either look at someone else and say "Zulu"—making them "it"—or can return the gaze of the first player and say "Micmac," which passes the ball back again. A second option for passing the ball back to the original "it" is to look at anyone other than the original "it" and say "Tally Ho." In both cases, the first player will again be "it." A fourth word, which may be used by whomsoever is "it", at anytime, is "Darwin." This makes the person two seats to the right of the speaker "it." In this case it doesn't matter what you are doing, it's simply where you *are* that gets you in trouble.

*ADELAIDE becomes fuddled.*

ADELAIDE    Oh doodle! – I simply don't understand "Darwin"!

*SILAS comes forward as Darwin.*

SILAS    (*English accent*) Any being, if it vary however slightly in any manner profitable to itself, under the complex and sometimes varying conditions of life, will have a better chance of surviving and thus be naturally selected.

ADELAIDE    I'm sorry?

ALICE    You were two seats to the right.

ADELAIDE    Oh.

KARL    You're still out. (*standing*) And furthermore, regarding Darwin...

## EUGENICS

*Light shift to KARL. A clock-like rhythm. Figures move in background – an automaton dance.*

KARL    There is now more to a raspberry than meets the eye. *(He is handed the bowl of raspberries which ALICE conjured earlier.)* I know a man in California who is breeding the best berries the world has ever tasted. He crossbreeds hundreds of varieties, takes a nibble of all of them, and simply destroys any that he doesn't like. It's quite a sight – millions upon millions of second-rate raspberries burning in great pits in the middle of his fields. But what he has left at the end of this process of selection is one very good berry. You see, Sir Charles Darwin has shown us how Nature destroys weaklings, and thanks to Darwin, we scientists are now able to tap Nature on the shoulder, and step into the dance ourselves.

But how? Well, if you begin with another science called biometrical statistics—which I invented—you can make everything mathematically predictable. You take real life, you plot it on a graph, and presto: it arranges itself into a "bell curve." A few stupid, ugly men on one end, lots of average men in the middle, and a handful of brilliant, beautiful men at the other extreme. It's predictable, like type in a drawer. But. It never changes. Not in our lifetimes. There was only one Newton, there is only one Faraday. So it seems tragic, doesn't it, that the brilliant end of the graph is doomed to be shallow. That our geniuses are always so few.

But what happens if we combine statistics with Darwin?

Aha! *That* is what we call eugenics – which I also invented. Or helped to invent. You see, if you take a population, and *breed* the best with best, you improve the population. It's simple. For smarter cities, breed Faradays. For more beautiful women, breed Antoinettes. All you do is plot your species on a bell curve, find out who's at the top, and breed them together. But it doesn't stop there. If you can breed for brains or beauty, then why not for strength and stamina? Well, you can. So why not for strength and stamina with *low* intelligence and short life span? What could be more helpful to a conquering race than to have at its disposal a docile race capable of great physical labour, that will not become a burden since it will never grow old? Nature can aid us in these quests, and the result will be science's greatest gift to the twentieth century.

> *A knock. The three other guests go off to investigate what this knock might be. KARL is left sitting, sneakily eating raspberries.*

**ALICE**     Dr. Pearson?

**KARL**      Yes?

**ALICE**     Did you take the raspberries in the loo with you?

**KARL**      Ah.... Well.

**ALICE**     I thought it might be you.

**KARL**      Sorry, it's just – Alice, how ever did you get hold of raspberries in the middle of a Canadian winter?

**ALICE**     Magic.

> *A clock chimes.*

## WAITING ROOM

> *The stage is empty but for the chairs. AUGUSTA enters. She sits. After a moment, KARL enters. The two pointedly ignore each other. KARL looks at his watch. Silence. After a moment, SILAS and ADELAIDE enter in friendly conversation. They are stopped mid-sentence by the stares of KARL and AUGUSTA. The chimes finish.*

# CHARADES

**ADELAIDE**  Ten o'clock – but we have contrived another idea to pass the time.

**KARL**  Is it brandy?

**ADELAIDE**  No, doctor, it isn't. It's a game I'm sure we all know.

**KARL**  Oh Lord, not another one.

**AUGUSTA**  It sounds delightful. What must we do, Adelaide?

**ADELAIDE**  First, form an audience–

> *They do, which situates ADELAIDE "on stage."*

**KARL**  But my sitting muscles–

**ADELAIDE**  –and the person who is before the audience–

**AUGUSTA**  That would be you!

**ADELAIDE**  So it is! That person must, without using any words, become a household object, such as a coo-coo clock, or a nutcracker!

> *ALICE enters from where she has been observing the above.*

**ALICE**  Oh, *good*! Charades!

> *SILAS slips away.*

**ADELAIDE**  I shall go first.

> *This is the most embarrassing, pathetic game ever witnessed. ADELAIDE performs a candle first.*

**KARL**  A glass of brandy.

**ADELAIDE**  Nooo–

**ALICE**  A chicken.

ADELAIDE    A household object, my dear.

KARL        A brandy snifter.

AUGUSTA     A weathervane.

ADELAIDE    No, no, I'm a candle!

KARL        (*to himself*) A candle.

> *Polite applause. AUGUSTA slips away.*

ADELAIDE    Try this one.

KARL        A large cigar.

ADELAIDE    Wait!

> *Now she attempts to become a pair of scissors.*

ALICE       An alligator.

ADELAIDE    *No* – a household object–

> *The players freeze as ALICE observes the following.*

## HATRED

AUGUSTA     A couple of years ago, a board—a board of men—decided it would be efficacious to close the Women's College Hospital. And I felt a particular *hatred* for the man that was the chair of that board. I won't name him. But I swear that I hated that man as much as I love my husband John. It was almost...

SILAS       Passionate.

AUGUSTA     Yes, I'm sorry. But it was passionate.

SILAS       Why are you thinking of this now?

AUGUSTA   I am afraid that I am thinking of all this because of
          Dr. Pearson. He is very much like that man in his
          certainty about the world. I think I feel hatred for
          Dr. Pearson.

SILAS     I imagine this is not an uncommon experience.
          (*beat*) But you don't, in fact, hate Dr. Pearson. You
          feel a strong revulsion to something in him that
          reminds you of this other experience.

AUGUSTA   That may be true, Reverend. But no, I think I hate
          Dr. Pearson. On his own merits.

SILAS     Well, yes. (*Pause.*) Dr. Stowe-Gullen – I have to
          admit that I am not an expert in the subject of
          women's advancement. I am a missionary, and
          I take my instruction from the Bible. It says there
          that woman is man's helpmeet. I cannot take that
          lightly, as much as I could not stand before a man
          who wished to commit adultery because he felt
          very strongly that he must. I hope you see my
          point.

AUGUSTA   You think I'm sinning.

SILAS     You are inflamed because men have tried to present
          the righteous path to you. And you have hated
          them for it. But they were not sinning in their
          actions. You have sinned in your *re*action. That is
          how I see it.

AUGUSTA   Well, Reverend. Thank you for listening to me. (*She
          exits.*)

SILAS     Of course.

          *Shift back to game of charades. ADELAIDE is
          exasperated with the others.*

ADELAIDE  No, no, no! I'm an egg beater! I'm making an
          omelette!

          *Polite applause. Ad lib commentary. They freeze.*

## AUGUSTA BREATHES FIRE

*A sudden flash: AUGUSTA enters and glares at the men. She breathes a mouthful of fire. ALICE observes all.*

## BOOKKEEPING

*Unfreeze. A shift of furniture.*

**ADELAIDE**   Let's each of us tell one joke. Only nothing more about corsets, Dr. Pearson.

**AUGUSTA**   Actually, John told me one this morning.

**ALICE**   *Excellent.*

**AUGUSTA**   Well, I wonder if I can remember it... let's see.... What's green, yellow, brown, and pink? (*beat*) A telephone. (*She mimes a phone.*) Green, green. Yellow? Sorry, brown number. (*She hangs up.*) Pink.

**ADELAIDE**   Wonderful!

**KARL**   Oh God.

**SILAS**   Brown number?

**ADELAIDE**   Alice? You must know a joke.

**ALICE**   You go first.

**ADELAIDE**   All right. What is the only word in the language to feature three double letters in a row?

**KARL**   Is this a joke?

**ALICE**   It's a riddle.

**SILAS**   Then the answer will be unexpected and amusing.

**ADELAIDE**   It will amuse, Reverend Rand—and I am glad you are paying attention—but there is a correct answer to the question.

**SILAS**      Then you are merely testing us, rather than providing a cause for laughter. If I recall correctly, a riddle is an enigmatic question designed to test the ingenuity of the listener–

**KARL**      (*quietly supportive*) Yes–

**SILAS**      Remembering a word is not the same as solving a riddle.

**KARL**      Quite right.

**AUGUSTA**      I confess I'm surprised at your vehemence, Reverend. And this, not even a religious issue.

**SILAS**      I abhor inaccuracy.

**ADELAIDE**      I see.

**KARL**      I have one. "Women and cats," says the young man, "are alike." "Wrong," replies his friend. "A woman can't run up a telegraph pole and a cat can't run up a millinery bill!"

> *Dead silence except for KARL, who quite enjoys his joke.*

**SILAS**      Strictly speaking, that was not a riddle either.

**KARL**      No. It was a joke.

**ADELAIDE**      Ah. It's funny, then, is it, to compare a woman to a cat?

**KARL**      Mrs. Hoodless, it is if it gets a laugh. Which I can see it did not.

**ADELAIDE**      If women run up millinery bills, it is to provide clothing for their families. I don't see what's funny about it.

**AUGUSTA**      I think it was meant lightly Adelaide.

**ADELAIDE**      I'm afraid I take it pointed.

**KARL**       Well, if my little joke gave offense, I apologise. But let me add that it seems unreasonable to make what is a woman's lot sound like an onerous and serious task. And I'm not categorizing, you understand, simply emphasizing what *is*.

**AUGUSTA**    Despite the fact that there is a woman doctor present.

**KARL**       Who likely has servants—women—who cook and mend her clothing for her. I'm not saying a man can't sew. I'm just saying a man doesn't. Women do, and women buy the fabric, hence: they run up millinery bills.

**AUGUSTA**    Is this still part of your apology?

**KARL**       Well, let's not make the darning of a sock sound as dangerous as coal-mining.

**ADELAIDE**   Dr. Pearson, I have sat around for over ninety minutes this evening and listened to you denigrate anything that is unfamiliar or unappealing to you, as if it is your main calling to disillusion anyone who doesn't see things the way you do.

**AUGUSTA**    Well put Adelaide.

**ADELAIDE**   Do you know that it is, in fact, dangerous to feed our infants milk? Plain milk, Dr. Pearson. While you are measuring the attributes of your race of perfect men and women, there are babies who are dead because no one taught their mothers how to heat milk. It's simple: having reached a temperature of thirty-two degrees centigrade, milk will cease to pose any kind of a threat to an infant. It is sweet and nourishing. At thirty-one degrees, however, it is potentially poison, full of lethal germs. One degree, Dr. Pearson. Can you measure that for us? Thirty-two and you wake up a family. Thirty-one and you have to call the casket-maker. Have *you* ever held one of your own children in your arms, watching the very life drain from its face? (*enormous grief*) Because you were feeding it poison and you didn't know any better? (*slight beat*) Or is that just women's work?...

*Huge silence. KARL is looking away.*

ALICE        (*carefully*) Bookkeeping.

             *Pause.*

ALICE        Bookkeeping. Two ohs, two kays, two ees. Bookkeeping.

ADELAIDE     Yes, Alice. That is the answer.

             *Pause.*

SILAS        It... was an excellent riddle, Mrs. Hoodless. An excellent. (*beat*) Riddle.

## THE GIFT OF JUNIPERS

*An up-tempo waltz. All except KARL drag their chairs off. KARL is left on stage. He is not happy. ALICE enters with a table covered with a piece of blue silk. She whips off the silk to reveal a bottle of gin and a glass. The music stops. She leaves. KARL sees the gin, dashes to table and downs a glassful. He sighs thankfully.*

KARL         Ohh, Yes!

*The waltz melody begins again with gusto. The others enter. There is a tray with a punch bowl. ALICE dances with KARL. SILAS dances with ADELAIDE. AUGUSTA is left with the tray. During the dance, KARL is able to pour all of the gin into the punch. The dance continues until...*

## ROLEPLAY

*Sudden light change. All on stage with glasses in hand. They are all slightly drunk, except ALICE.*

ALICE          (*to SILAS*) Now you're to be Dr. Stowe-Gullen, (*to ADELAIDE*) and you will play Reverend Rand. The topic is mutton. Ready – Go!

> *The four characters have been assigned each other as roles. They each have props or bits of costume to better play one another. Their acting is alarmingly large.*

KARL           (*as ADELAIDE*) Who would like another piece of mutton!

SILAS          (*as AUGUSTA*) I think we should vote on who gets the last piece! All in favour!

AUGUSTA        (*as KARL*) Well, I think the men can probably solve that little problem on their own!

SILAS          (*as AUGUSTA*) How unfair! How unfair! I will stamp my feet and grind my teeth in protest!

ADELAIDE       (*as SILAS*) I should like to take the mutton for the poor and the needy.

> *They all suddenly drop character.*

KARL           Mrs. Hoodless, really. If you can't sink your teeth into it, perhaps you should sit out.

SILAS          I think it was an accurate portrayal.

KARL           But not a parody. I get "count the women out" and you get "feed the poor?" I don't think so. Alice, make Dr. Stowe-Gullen play Reverend Rand, and Mrs. Hoodless can play me.

ADELAIDE       Oh, I don't think I should.

ALICE          I think it's an excellent idea.

KARL           Yes, so do I.

ALICE          All right, begin again.

> *Beat.*

AUGUSTA    (*as SILAS*) Anyone who is Christian may have a
           piece of mutton, but those that aren't can starve!

SILAS      (*as AUGUSTA*) You nasty man! Can't you see since
           the women made the mutton, they should get all of
           it!

AUGUSTA    (*as SILAS*) Why feed people who have no share in
           the next world! There is no mutton in Hell, anyway.

KARL       (*an aside to SILAS*) See? That's much better!
           (*as ADELAIDE*) Oh my! That's awfully cruel! Oh
           doodle! I think I shall cry a river. Oh boo hoo!
           (*waiting*) Well, Dr. Pearson, don't you think it cruel?

ADELAIDE   (*as KARL*) Oh, um, no. It's not cruel. In fact, I think
           all those people who don't deserve mutton should
           be killed forthright. And also all the people who get
           mutton, especially if they're Christians, and they
           should be killed with knives and hammers and left
           to bleed by the side of the road, and also women,
           should be killed, just... hacked apart like sacks of
           garbage set upon by dogs. Everyone should be
           killed but me! I am the only one who should live!!

           *Silence.*

KARL       That's a little harsh, Mrs. Hoodless.

ADELAIDE   Oh. Well, I guess I just don't know how to play this
           little game.

           *The others stifle laughter.*

           *KARL is left alone on stage. An abandoned little
           boy.*

### SONG: DO YE KEN JOHN PEEL

           *All re-enter singing while looking disparagingly
           at KARL.*

Do ye ken John Peel with his coat so gay?
Do ye ken John Peel at the break of day?
Do ye ken John Peel when he's far, far away?
With his fox and his hounds in the morning?

*They exit as the music continues.*

## SONG: DO YE KEN GOLDWIN SMITH

> *This parody of "John Peel" follows the previous song in time. It is KARL being unpleasant. He sings:*

Do ye ken Goldwin Smith when he's four hours late?
Do ye ken Goldwin Smith when you wait, wait, wait?
Do ye ken Goldwin Smith when you sing songs you hate?
And you're trapped with a pack of chatt'ring monkeys.

> *ALICE takes his punch glass away from him. The others are suddenly back on stage.*

## FAITH BY CANDLELIGHT

**AUGUSTA**  Look, we've got about an hour until midnight. We can't go anywhere else given the weather, and I can only assume that our host will not let us suffer the New Year without him. So let's try to make the last moments of the century memorable ones. There is no reason why a talented group such as ourselves cannot truly have a fine evening on our own. Now *I* have an idea for a game.

**ADELAIDE**  Really, Augusta?

**AUGUSTA**  Yes, Adelaide. And it is nominally competitive, so I think even the men will enjoy it. Is there a candle?

**ALICE**  A candle.

*Magically, a candle appears from the wings.*
*ALICE takes it and hands it to AUGUSTA.*

**AUGUSTA**    And perhaps a square of cloth?

*ALICE magically produces a long piece of blue silk fabric.*

**ALICE**    I have a scarf.

*The candle is placed on a table, and lighted.*

**AUGUSTA**    Very simply, once blindfolded, you must find your way to the candle and blow it out.

**ALICE**    Perfect! I'll go first.

*ALICE is blindfolded. She is placed directly in front of the candle.*

**AUGUSTA**    Now take three steps back... and turn around three times... and now walk forward and blow out the candle.

*ALICE attempts this and is wildly off.*

**ALICE**    That wasn't very good.

**AUGUSTA**    Well, it's certainly not a problem with lung capacity.

**ALICE**    No, it's not my stays. I was just awful.

**AUGUSTA**    Dr. Pearson?

**KARL**    Oh no. I would like to watch again. You know, learn from others.

**ADELAIDE**    Well Dr. Pearson... I am a teacher in real life, so keep your eye on me.

*ADELAIDE is given a turn. She walks directly towards SILAS, in effect cornering him, and ends up blowing in his face – despite his efforts to avoid her.*

**ADELAIDE**   (*lifting the blindfold*) Oh.

**SILAS**   Tell me, Mrs. Hoodless, how close you thought you were.

**ADELAIDE**   (*embarrassed*) I felt I was very close indeed.

**ALICE**   Why do you ask, Reverend?

**SILAS**   Because it strikes me that the game is a metaphor for faith.

**KARL**   Is it.

**SILAS**   We close our eyes and seek out the light.

**KARL**   And then try to blow it out.

**SILAS**   Well, that part of the game is heretical.

**KARL**   Alright, enough of this: put the blindfold on me.

> *KARL is blindfolded and led to the table.*

**AUGUSTA**   No cheating, Karl Pearson! I can think of ingenious ways you might cheat.

**ADELAIDE**   No fluttering of the garments!

**ALICE**   No holding your hands out to feel for the heat!

**SILAS**   I think with Dr. Pearson, the candle may just go out as he approaches.

**KARL**   In obeisance to his powers, you mean!

**SILAS**   In resignation.

> *KARL feels his way with genuine attention. But he actually wanders off stage. A crash is heard. KARL screams. General amusement. KARL re-enters, glaring.*

**KARL**   Right. Well. Next.

*They all now look to the REVEREND.*

ALICE        Reverend – won't you please try?

SILAS        I feel uneasy about participating.

ADELAIDE     Just think, in about sixty minutes, you can say it
             happened back in the nineteenth century.

SILAS        Very well. I'm here, aren't I?

             *He is blindfolded and placed in front of the table.*

SILAS        The metaphor of faith is that man does not try to
             find God, but that he is drawn to God.

             *His three turns are breathtaking, and SILAS is
             drawn without hesitation to the candle. He leans
             down and his mouth is exactly one inch away
             from the flame. Although, he does not extinguish
             it.*

ALICE        Gosh.

KARL         For goodness sake.

ADELAIDE     Are you going to take your turn, Reverend Rand?

             *SILAS recites an appropriate prayer in Latin:*

SILAS        *Sicuti sum – nec sine spe,*
             *Quia Tu mortuus es pro me,*
             *O Agnus Dei, venio.*

             *He then blows gently. The stage is plunged into
             darkness.*

## THE STORY SO FAR

             *Lights come up on ALICE, standing alone on
             stage.*

ALICE        Here's the story so far: A young girl, sent to
             entertain four party guests on the eve of a new

century, succeeds with a variety of games. No.
Four argumentative older persons find themselves
at a party without a host and – unable to leave, they
begin to squabble like geese. No. A blue silk scarf
is produced from about the person of a sweet
young girl, a girl of both admirable character
and fantastically beguiling appearance, and, as
the clock strikes twelve...

> *She conjures a bouquet of flowers. Again, she is*
> *surprised by her own magic.*

Peonies! How lovely!

## SONG: PENNYWORTH OF PREENS

> *A dance of candlelight.*

> *The men sing the first verse:*

**MEN**      I'll give you a pennyworth of preens,
That's aye the way that love begins.
If you'll walk with me, lady.
If you'll walk with me, lady.

> *The women now sing.*

**WOMEN**    I'll no hae your pennyworth of preens,
That's no the way that love begins.
And I'll no walk with you, with you.
I'll no walk with you, with you.

## NAKEDNESS

> *AUGUSTA standing in a pool of light. Part way*
> *through her speech, ALICE appears, dimly lit*
> *upstage of her, and begins dancing, as if to*
> *AUGUSTA's words.*

**AUGUSTA**   Leave the lights on, he says. It's been a year, we've
already... been husband and wife. But he says, leave
the lights on, and I laugh, I say John, just... turn

them off. Leave a candle on, but I'm not having the bulb burning overhead the whole time. It's silly. He comes over and kisses me. Auggie, you've seen bodies, what's the problem? Dead bodies, I say to him, dead bodies. Well this is nicer says John, I'm actually pink and red and ruddy. And he takes off his shirt, his collar, his cuffs. His shoes, his socks and garters. Undoes his belt. Come on, John, shut the light, but I'm laughing, and I'm... enjoying it. Then his suspenders, snap snap, his undershirt. And then his trousers and then – well. Then, then he's naked, my John. He comes over, I have pins and needles in my palm, like there's going to be a thunderstorm. He undoes my green collar and slips it out, then unbuttons the lavender pure taffeta silk waist and lets it fall to the ground. Then he pulls off the all-wool Moreen Black underskirt and snaps the six hooks on my Armorside summer corset, pulling open the bows on the Kabo Bust Perfector, revealing me in my handsome four tuck Nainsook drawers with its ruffle of Hamburg embroidery, beneath which is my... (*Pause.*) Oh my. Then we're standing there and I wonder, where's the apple I'm supposed to hand him? And I'm shaking like a school girl. Like a girl.

**ALICE**      (*softly*) What happens next?

**AUGUSTA**    (*lights fading out*) Well, we... and then we... during which we... thrice. And then we...

## A CONDOM!

*Another oddly lit moment.*

**KARL**       I prefer the woman superior... in bed! It frees one's hands.

**ADELAIDE**   (*bravely*) "Smile and think of England!"

**SILAS**      Loose fitting undergarments can produce random tumescence. Ahem.

AUGUSTA    Postponement of procreation provides pure
           pleasure.

           *A condom, circa 1899, is lowered from above.*
           *They gather around it.*

ALICE      What is this?

AUGUSTA    It is a con-dome.

SILAS      Ohhhh–

           *SILAS faints and the women attend to him.*
           *A rhythm begins as the lights shift.*


## THE TEMPTATION OF SILAS RAND

           *A fever dream.*

SILAS      The women. The women, city women. In muslin
           dresses and silk gloves. Lord, the flesh of women,
           the warmth of women. Am I sinning to have these
           thoughts? Yes – more than Saint Augustine, yes
           much more. But why else do I find myself here on
           this day, with these unusual companions if not to
           confront this desire? Do I not secretly want to live
           in a city among fashionable Christians, drinking
           their liquors with them, walking home among the
           leaves to a fire and a wife with a kind face, a good
           heart? And a soft belly, and warm round breasts?
           Do I not desire these things even more than they
           do? (*realising*) Thank You, Lord Jesus, thank You
           Father on high for this trial. I will deny, deny,
           deny...

ALICE      (*stepping into his light*) Silas. Why dost thou give up
           so easily? Why not convert the white man of the
           city, and leaveth the poor savage to his forest? Then
           wilt thou have that warm house, and feel thy wife's
           buttocks pushing against thee.

SILAS      That is the choice of a weak man ready for
           fattening.

ALICE      Art thou saying comfort with what the Lord
           provideth and the happiness of physical love is
           not good enough for Silas Rand?

SILAS      No, I–

ALICE      Dost not God's light fall on me as well? Is not
           mine body part of the earthly bounty? Put thy
           lips on mine–

SILAS      No–

ALICE      Am not I thy Mary Magdalene?

SILAS      No, it isn't you, it wasn't you I was thinking of.

ALICE      What? Then whom?

           *AUGUSTA appears, as ALICE recedes.*

AUGUSTA    She is too young for a man of thy experience.
           Slake thy thirst on one full of her years, satisfy thy
           passion at her hands. Thou wert thinking of me.

SILAS      No, I was not–

           *ADELAIDE appears, as AUGUSTA recedes.*

SILAS      ...it is she.

ADELAIDE   *Me?* Why do I tempt you Silas? I'm not young any
           more. I'm not beautiful and I never was. I am...
           ashamed of my body. I can't be the one who
           tempts you.

SILAS      But you are good. You are good. I can tell you
           would be kind, you would be patient. You would
           not draw me away from the path. Lord God, free
           me from these thoughts!

           *Pause.*

## THINGS THAT GO BUMP IN THE NIGHT

> *Quick light shift to SILAS and ADELAIDE, bumping into each other. ALICE watches from behind.*

**SILAS**  Oh, sorry.

**ADELAIDE**  No, I bumped into you.

> *They narrowly avoid bumping into each other again. They laugh. ADELAIDE exits. SILAS has a moment of quiet before he follows her off.*

## THE FAIR LADY

> *A strange light. ALICE sings while SILAS and ADELAIDE enter upstage and begin dancing together.*

**ALICE**  As I went by the Luckenbooths, I saw a lady fair.
She had lang pendles in her ears, and jewels in her hair.
And when she came to our door, she spiered at who was ben, [*She inquired who was within.*]
"Oh, hae ye seen my lost love with his braw Highland men?"
The smile about her bonnie cheek was sweeter than the bee.
Her voice was like the birdie's sang upon the birken tree.
But when the minister came out, her mare began to prance.
They rode into the sunset, beyond the coast of France.

## JERUSALEM

> *Lights return to normal. SILAS and ADELAIDE are sharing a laugh.*

**ADELAIDE**  I feel this whole evening you have hidden your light under a barrel.

SILAS          I only have a little light, Mrs. Hoodless, and it is
               best seen in the dark.

ADELAIDE       (*misunderstanding*) I beg your pardon?

SILAS          When you are leading people out of darkness, even
               the dimmest light will do.

ADELAIDE       Oh! (*relieved*) Oh yes.

SILAS          But you are a good person, Mrs. Hoodless. You are
               good. I feel... like you are the only one I can talk to
               here. This is a trial for me, you know.

ADELAIDE       I feel as if this is a trial for each of us, in a peculiar
               way. You know, when you told your story of the
               three kings, I thought for a moment you were
               telling us about yourself.

SILAS          Perhaps I was, yes. One loves a story for personal
               reasons I suppose.

ADELAIDE       Silas, I have dreamt of you.

               *He looks at her. He might fall to his knees if he's
               not careful.*

ADELAIDE       I didn't know who it was until you told your story,
               but I dreamt of a man sleeping among stands of
               wheat. He opens his eyes when I look down at him
               and he smiles. I tell him the worst has passed.

SILAS          What is the worst?

ADELAIDE       That there is no God walking beside you, nor no
               love from those in your care. And no-one to take
               care of you in your later years. That all you built
               will turn to dust.

SILAS          When did you have this dream?

ADELAIDE       Just a couple of nights ago. I remember it vividly.
               I think I was a messenger, and I was telling you the
               worst had passed. You were written at that moment
               into the book of life.

*They stand looking into each other's eyes.*

(*spellbound, quietly*) What do you think it means?

SILAS  (*quietly*) I don't know. Perhaps it means sanctuary after many trials. Our journey towards... well (*Pause.*) Jerusalem.

> *A version of the hymn "Jerusalem" is heard.*
> *SILAS and ADELAIDE exit. ALICE enters from*
> *where she has been watching them. She is trying*
> *to perform another magic trick. This time, she*
> *produces a directional lantern, circa 1899, from*
> *under her silk handkerchief. She is puzzled by this.*

ALICE  Hmm.

## WHEN SHADOWS SHAKE HANDS

*All are seated.*

KARL  *Well.* I have been sitting here for a very long time. So I think an entire gallon of gin would be a suitable reward, seeing as how I have been such a good boy.

ALICE  (*placing her finger beside her nose*) I don't know, Dr. Pearson. What do you think, Mrs. Hoodless?

ADELAIDE  (*noting ALICE's finger, places one beside her own nose*) Oh, I don't know, Alice.

ALICE  Ah, Dr. Stowe-Gullen – should we fetch Dr. Pearson a gallon of gin?

AUGUSTA  (*twigging, placing a finger beside her nose*) Would a gallon be enough?

KARL  (*looks up*) Now *that* is an excellent question – what are you all doing?

ALICE  (*vehemently gesturing to SILAS*) Reverend – what do *you* think?

| | |
|---|---|
| **SILAS** | I abstain from discussions of alcohol. |
| **ALICE** | No Reverend... what do you *think*. |
| **SILAS** | Oh for goodness sake. (*He pointedly places a finger beside his nose.*) |
| **ALICE** | (*triumphant, to KARL*) Aha! You lose! |
| **KARL** | Really. |
| **ALICE** | You must pay a forfeit. |
| **KARL** | I think my punishment should be that I be sent back to my hotel. |
| **AUGUSTA** | No – the punishment must be suitable. Something that fits the forfeiter. |
| **ADELAIDE** | I know! |
| **KARL** | Oh God. |
| **ADELAIDE** | You'll find this dear, Dr. Pearson. I command you to kiss your own shadow! |
| **KARL** | I beg your pardon? |
| **ADELAIDE** | Alice do you have a lantern? |
| **ALICE** | Yes, I do. |
| **ADELAIDE** | Dr. Pearson, I will hold the lantern behind your head, and you must endeavour to kiss your own shadow. |
| **AUGUSTA** | How inventive, Adelaide! |
| **KARL** | Under no circumstances– |
| **ALICE** | Oh do it for me! |

*A beat. Then KARL acquiesces silently.*

| | |
|---|---|
| **ALICE** | Wonderful. |

**ADELAIDE**   Let's dim one or two of these lights.

> *Some of the lights are dimmed, and ADELAIDE*
> *comes behind KARL, bearing a lantern.*
> *ADELAIDE holds the lantern in such a way*
> *as to cast KARL's shadow on the floor.*

**KARL**   Very clever, Mrs. Hoodless.

> *KARL gets down on his hands and knees to kiss*
> *his shadow, but, at the last moment, ADELAIDE*
> *moves the shadow away.*

I see. This could go on.

> *Ad lib laughter and dialogue. KARL's shadow*
> *is thrown across the room, and ADELAIDE*
> *manœuvers the lantern and her relation to KARL*
> *in such a way as to make the shadow smaller and*
> *bring it across ALICE's face. ALICE is merely*
> *watching what is happening and doesn't realize*
> *that ADELAIDE is manufacturing a kiss between*
> *herself and KARL. At the last instant, KARL sees*
> *his shadow on ALICE's face. There is a moment of*
> *tense expectation.*

Oh. I'm sorry...

**ALICE**   Wait!

> *She grabs his face and draws him in for a*
> *passionate kiss. The rest of the characters have*
> *frozen. When she draws back from him, he's*
> *frozen as well.*

**ALICE**   (*to the audience*) Well. (*She shrugs.*) But I don't think
it will help. Poor man.

> *Then the scene resumes from right before that*
> *moment.*

**KARL**   (*somewhat confused*) Oh. I'm sorry...

**ALICE**   No, that's quite alright.

**KARL**   Uh, right.

**ALICE**   Play on.

**KARL**   (*to ADELAIDE*) Yes, play on...

> *The game continues. ADELAIDE causes KARL's shadow to fall across AUGUSTA's face. AUGUSTA shrieks in mock horror and evades him.*

**KARL**   Very funny, Dr. Stowe-Gullen.

> *The light swirls around. The shadows dance. Finally the shadow lands on SILAS.*

**KARL**   Perhaps I should just *shake* my shadow's hand.

**SILAS**   An excellent idea, considering.

**KARL**   Shadow.

**SILAS**   Shadow.

> *They shake, and immediately, they lock hands and begin turning in a slow, antagonistic circle. The lights shift.*

### THE TEST

*A dance for the two men.*

**KARL**   Missionaries. You should drop your Micmac bibles and run. The Indians, the niggers, the yellow man... none of them will ever be the white man, no matter how many pipes you smoke with them.

**SILAS**   And you, scaling the wall and launching yourself at the face of God! You hobbyist. You ought to be counting ducks in city ponds, isn't that what statistics was created for? Not rearranging their genetic material. You are nipping at your Master's heels.

KARL      *Wer immerdar nach Schatten greift,*
*Kann stets nur leere Luft erlangen:*
*Wer Schatten stets auf Schatten häuft,*
*Sieht endlich sich von düstrer Nacht umfangen.*

Well? (*beat*)

SILAS      A man who is always snatching at shadows will never grasp anything but air; he who piles shadow upon shadow will find himself trapped in endless night.

> *A shift in light. What has been a wrestling match is now simply a handshake.*

SILAS      Goethe, I believe.

KARL      Very good, Dr. Rand. And an excellent translation.

SILAS      *Danke, Herr Pearson.* I may believe in God, but I am not an idiot, as you can see.

KARL      Yes. Evolution allows for all sorts of contradictions.

## SONG: WELL RUNG TOM BOY

> *The others enter for a round, sung by all.*

Well rung Tom boy, well rung Tom.
Well rung, cuckoo, well rung Tom.
The owl and the cuckoo, the fool and the song,
Well sung, cuckoo, well rung Tom.

> *All exit except ALICE and AUGUSTA.*

## MARY

> *ALICE is seated. AUGUSTA is brushing her hair.*

ALICE      Tom Sawyer? You must be joking... now I remind you of *Tom Sawyer?*

AUGUSTA      But I, *admire* those qualities, those free-spirited qualities you have, just like that young boy–

| | |
|---|---|
| **ALICE** | He wore torn trousers! |
| **AUGUSTA** | Well, no, you are much better dressed, all I mean is his brilliant scheming – you're very bold... |
| **ALICE** | But I thought I reminded you of your friend, Mary, from England. |
| **AUGUSTA** | Alice, why are you so interested in Mary? |
| **ALICE** | Forgive me, Dr. Stowe-Gullen, but I can't tell you... I mean, I can't... begin to tell you how curious I am. |
| **AUGUSTA** | I was the same, at your age. |
| **ALICE** | It must be difficult knowing she's in prison. |
| **AUGUSTA** | Yes. It is. |
| **ALICE** | Do you worry about her terribly? |
| **AUGUSTA** | Yes. I do. |
| **ALICE** | Have you heard from her? I mean since she began her... |
| **AUGUSTA** | Hunger strike. |
| **ALICE** | Yes. |
| **AUGUSTA** | It's odd you should ask, I got a letter yesterday. |
| **ALICE** | Tell me. |
| **AUGUSTA** | Let's talk rather of Mr. Twain. He is a guilty pleasure... |
| **ALICE** | No. (*She takes AUGUSTA's hand.*) Tell me about Mary. |
| **AUGUSTA** | (*beat, not sure at first*) She... well, she wrote to me that every day she is strapped to a chair by four or five matronly women – twice her size, and seemingly delighted not to have the vote. And then a doctor, such as myself, but probably a man... feeds her against her will. |

ALICE     But why doesn't she just keep her mouth closed?

          *AUGUSTA gently touches ALICE's nose.*

AUGUSTA   They put it in her nose. A rubber feeding tube—that
          is larger in diameter than the nostril into which it is
          forced—is pushed into her nose and down the back
          of her throat, to her stomach. She wants to vomit,
          but she can't. She's in pain, but she's strapped
          down. She's helpless. That is how they keep the
          good women of Britain from starving themselves.
          Alice.

ALICE     Oh.

          *Shift. AUGUSTA is addressing a lecture theatre.
          ALICE is a "demonstration" of a force-feeding
          victim.*

AUGUSTA   The human esophagus is made up of three layers—
          an inner mucous membrane, a middle or areolar
          membrane, and an outer muscular sheath. To feed
          a subject who is unwilling to eat, a rubber tube is
          inserted in the nasal cavity and deployed over the
          soft palette, down the gullet, and towards her
          stomach. This tube needs to be fairly rigid to avoid
          collapse, so, within the esophagus, the mucous
          membrane is usually scraped away—the subject
          will end up digesting it—the middle membrane is
          perforated, and the muscle sheath, all the while
          attempting to vomit the tube up, is left bruised and
          torn. The resultant scarring, or fibrous cicatrisation
          of the esophagus, will produce what we call
          stricture, or gradual blockage. Odynophagia or
          disphagia will follow. In other words the subject
          will have trouble swallowing, or will experience
          pain even while taking tea and toast for the rest of
          her life. Now. Once the tube hits bottom, a funnel is
          placed into the outside end, and a mixture of raw
          eggs and milk is poured in; at this point the subject
          will convulse involuntarily, hence the presence of
          leather straps—firmly secured at the beginning of
          the procedure. When the feeding is complete, the
          tube is simply pulled out – a task aided by the

ongoing parystalsis in the subject's throat. A cloth is
used to stem the flow of blood and other fluids
from the nasal cavity, the leather straps are released
and the subject is free to go back to her cell. Unless,
of course, she vomits, in which case the entire
procedure is repeated.

*Shift back.*

You see, Alice. They torture her. Like a traitor. All
because Mary wants to mark a little "x" on a little
piece of paper.

ALICE        You love her very much.

AUGUSTA      Yes, Alice. My heart is broken.

### GAME: MINISTER'S CAT

*All play. They are seated, and use their hands to
thump out a rhythm on their knees. They're on
"H".*

KARL         The minister's cat is a hopeless cat.

SILAS        The minister's cat is a heavenly cat.

AUGUSTA      The minister's cat is a hungry cat.

ADELAIDE     The minister's cat is a happy cat.

*Etcetera.*

ALICE        In the game called The Minister's Cat, a group of
people use a single letter from the alphabet to
define what kind of cat the minister has. It's a fast
game, and you forfeit the right to play if you
stumble, repeat yourself, or simply fail to keep up.
You are also eliminated once your imagination,
education, or even your grammar fails you.

SILAS        The Minister's cat is *not* heathenous.

KARL            Ha. You're out!

ADELAIDE        No, Dr. Pearson: that was an incorrect use of "hea-
                then." You're out.

KARL            I think I know the correct use of a heathen. (*He
                enjoys his little joke.*)

SILAS           I'm sure you do, Doctor Pearson. But in *this* case, it
                is a noun. It has no adjectival form, hence it cannot
                modify "cat." You have made a mistake.

KARL            Impossible.

AUGUSTA         (*delighted*) Dr. Pearson, I believe you have earned a
                forfeit.

KARL            (*heated*) No! Heathenous is *most certainly* a–

ALICE           Dr. Pearson! (*He stands sheepishly.*) You must now
                tell us all something we do not know.

KARL            There's too much to choose from.

ALICE           (*reprimanding him*) Dr. Pearson.

### THE MAN IN A BOX

> *A Relativity dance. KARL is in the centre. The
> others surround him.*

KARL            All right. I think I have just the thing. Imagine... a
                man in a box. This box he is in is floating in space,
                and the man inside the box is also floating within
                the box. There is an apple floating in the air beside
                him and on his other side, a cannonball floats just
                as lightly as the apple. Now, a cosmic demon comes
                along outside, attaches a chain to the top of the box
                and gives it an almighty pull. Inside the box, the
                floor rushes up to meet the man's feet, and the
                apple and the cannonball smash into the floor on
                either side of him as the demon continues to pull.
                Now this man has studied Newton–

**AUGUSTA**   Aha! So he hasn't always been in a box–

**KARL**   No, at some pre-boxal time he has read Newton and he has noticed that all of the floating objects of differing mass, including himself, met the floor at the same rate of speed. So what conclusion does he make?

**ALICE**   He thinks it's gravity.

**KARL**   Yes. That is correct.

**ALICE**   So he thinks he's fallen to the floor.

**ADELAIDE**   Wait a second.... He doesn't realise... he doesn't realise the floor has come up to him.

**KARL**   Exactly!

**SILAS**   (*carefully*) Even though... he has not moved himself, he believes that he has suddenly acquired weight and gone crashing to the floor.

**KARL**   It's known as the Man-in-the-Box paradigm. You see? This is the new science. It will be called "relativity." From now on, what you see will not tell you what is *actually* going on.

**ADELAIDE**   (*behind KARL*) And...

> *Here each speaker steps behind the person whose point of view they are espousing, sticking their arms through the elbows of the person in front. The one in front mimes the words being spoken as their "fake" arms gesticulate.*

...the principles inherent in genetic engineering will considerably enhance our enjoyment of life.

**SILAS**   (*behind AUGUSTA*) And making women equal partners in the political process will effect an advance in human rights!

**KARL**   (*behind ADELAIDE*) Not to mention that offering men and women defined social roles will create a

nurturing society where respect for individuals will
be commonplace.

AUGUSTA    (*behind SILAS*) And of course, God is the moral glue
that will direct us all to good works, no matter
what our calling!

ADELAIDE   How exciting this is!

ALICE      It's a magic box.

    *An apple falls from above, which ALICE catches.*

And you're all in it.

    *A cannonball rolls in a leisurely way across the*
    *stage.*

## SONG: LINGLE LINGLE LANG TANG

    *An Ode to Schrödinger.*

    *All sing.*

ALL        Lingle lingle lang tang, our cat's died.
What did she die with? With a sore head.
All you that kent her when she was alive,
Come to her burial atween four and five.

## NINETEEN NINETY NINE

    *They are all seated in the parlour once again.*

ALICE      Alright, I have another idea. I propose we go
around and describe the scene on New Year's Eve
one hundred years ago. What do you think people
were wishing for?

KARL       Indoor plumbing.

ALICE      Dr. Pearson. Take this seriously. Please.

KARL       Well, for one thing, the world was a very different
place one hundred years ago. They knew nothing of

what we call modern. No Rutherford. No Edison.
In fact, they had rather bizarre notions of what
everything was made of, names for elements like
"ponderous earth."

AUGUSTA    And do you suppose the earth is no longer
ponderous?

KARL    A theory is only as good as its usefulness. That one
is now useless. But I think they were most likely
just sitting about on their hands waiting for
Darwin.

ADELAIDE    Honestly.

KARL    And those that weren't were busy building
churches.

SILAS    (*an old hat at KARL's jibes now*) Most of which are
still standing to this day. A church is not a theory,
Karl.

KARL    *Touché*, Silas.

AUGUSTA    I don't think people were so very different. My
grandmother was marrying my grandfather in
1799. And little did they know what they would
produce.

ADELAIDE    Lady doctors as far as the eye can see.

KARL    It's genetic is it?

ALICE    This question is too easy. Tell me about a hundred
years from now. New Year's Eve, 1999?

KARL    Those immortals? They'll be toasting the globe from
the surface of Mars.

ALICE    Yes. But what else?

> *Light change. The characters will stand on their
> lines and state them flatly outwards.*

AUGUSTA   In the twentieth century, women will lead their nations.

SILAS   In the twentieth century, there will be bold new religions.

KARL   People will be numbered for identification.

ADELAIDE   In the twentieth century, household appliances will do away with unwanted children.

>   *Faster.*

SILAS   In the twentieth century, God will have his own house on the coast.

ADELAIDE   There will be water merchants.

KARL   *Some* vegetables will be eaten raw. (*The others shudder.*)

>   *Very fast now.*

AUGUSTA   In the twentieth century, there will be–

SILAS   A lot of rubbish.

KARL   You will need a key–

ADELAIDE   For everything.

SILAS   People will keep their teeth–

AUGUSTA   For their whole lives.

ADELAIDE   (*topping them all*) In the twentieth century, it will be legal for women to go about topless!

>   *A beat.*

ALL   What?

ADELAIDE   You know, shirtless.

KARL   Really.

*Resume.*

**SILAS**    In the twentieth century, the soul will be dried out, crushed into powder and sold in stores.

**KARL**    There will be no more Muslims or Jews.

**ADELAIDE**    Everyone will wear a protective sheathe.

**AUGUSTA**    Men will have their penises widened and learn to give birth.

**KARL**    Ouch.

**ADELAIDE**    In the twentieth century, the corporate culture will provide a measure of stability to an ever-increasing population, thus ensuring a good wage for all peoples, a comfortable environment, and an atmosphere of mutual respect and caring.

*Beat.*

**ALL**    In the twentieth century...

**ALICE**    You will all be dead.

*Beat. Light change back. The characters sit.*

**AUGUSTA**    Alice? What is your fancy?

**ALICE**    On the eve of the twenty-first century, I see the women, living on one side of the ocean, sending New Year's greetings to the men, three thousand miles away on the other side. And the men will eagerly receive this greeting—many of them will still be able to remember the women, you see—and some of them will say, Goodness, the women seem to be doing quite well.

**AUGUSTA**    (*laughing*) And that is your planet one hundred years from now?

**ALICE**    I've seen it so many times in my mind's eye.

KARL        Well, if you're going to invoke the scientific method–

ALICE       The men will have moved away, having agreed with the women that they needed a space to build things in, and they will have built these things, oh a great many things, and will be fighting over them, which is also something they needed, else they began to feel piqued and discouraged. And the women will simply be planting gardens. They will have turned their whole continent lush with greenery and flowers. And they will send great boatloads of peonies over to the men. And the men will say, My, the women do seem to be doing extremely well.

KARL        Aha – but who will conduct the boats?

ALICE       (*thinking*) Eunuchs.

ADELAIDE  And what of families?

ALICE       People together in one place will still be families.

AUGUSTA  And your new, dualised species – how will it propagate?

ALICE       This is the interesting part: the women will learn to pollinate each other—very gently, you understand, perhaps over tea—and the men will begin to divide like amoebas.

SILAS       Goodness.

KARL        You posit an earth where the men reproduce at exponentially increasing rates, where the women, one assumes, evolve somewhat more chaotically, and with greater genetic variability.

ALICE       No: the men split apart and the women mix.

AUGUSTA  They become many and we become one.

ALICE       Yes. That's how I see the future.

**AUGUSTA**     Interesting.

**ADELAIDE**    Sad.

**KARL**        Preposterous.

**SILAS**       And what happens to God? Is He a "he" in this world?

**ALICE**       I haven't figured out God yet, Reverend. I think, what God was, before this, was the men and the women mixed together. So, in the future, there is no God.

            *Pause.*

**SILAS**       You believe this?

**ALICE**       Yes.

**ADELAIDE**    How horrible.

**SILAS**       And probably true.

### DEATH

*ALICE stands alone on a dimly lit stage and surveys the chairs in which the others had just been sitting. These chairs have all been knocked over, and are now empty. She wanders among them and a strange melody is heard – perhaps a version of "Auld Lang Syne."*

### AN EXPLOSION

*Lights up.*

**KARL**        (*mid-rant*) Well for God's sake it seems obvious your Uncle isn't coming! Perhaps he never intended to. And if we have one more song, riddle, or game, I shall begin to haemorrhage! So, Miss Alice, I must ask you: why have we been brought here tonight? What is the point of detaining four decent human beings for no apparent reason!

ALICE        You spoiled Musical Chairs.

KARL         I am asking you a question.

ALICE        I'm sure I don't know. I didn't realise you were
             being "detained."

KARL         Well, we are. Detained, and I daresay tricked.
             And we will sit here until you provide a suitable
             explanation.

ADELAIDE     Dr. Pearson, there is no need to bully the girl.

ALICE        All I know is that Uncle told me I should take care
             of his friends for him while he was delayed.

KARL         Take care of! With hardly a biscuit or a spirit to
             wash it down with! He meant for you to strain us
             to our very limits! Our very limits!!

AUGUSTA      And who said we were friends, Alice? I only came
             so that I might finally answer your uncle to his
             face for those vile articles of his. He's no friend of
             mine. Nor is he of Adelaide's, I believe, though he
             mistakenly finds her harmless.

ADELAIDE     Oh, Augusta. What does it matter anymore. He's
             not coming.

SILAS        He is *my* friend. He sent me money to visit my
             dying brother.

KARL         He probably poisoned him.

ADELAIDE     No host. No family. No friends.

SILAS        Mrs. Hoodless...

ADELAIDE     Abandoned on New Year's Eve.

KARL         Stop your prating, woman.

AUGUSTA      Dr. Pearson!

**ADELAIDE**   A fitting punishment for our pride, don't you think, Karl?

**KARL**   Will you *shut up*!

**SILAS**   (*low, threatening*) That is enough, Karl Pearson.

**KARL**   Reverend. Dr. Stowe-Gullen. Mrs. Hoodless. Does it not seem odd to you that we four have been stranded together on a night where I'm sure we'd all rather be elsewhere? All I want to know is *why*. Alice?!

**ALICE**   I... I can't say. It's too...

**KARL**   Nonsense! You *can* and you *will*, or you shall be very, very sorry young lady.

**AUGUSTA**   Oh for God's sake!

**KARL**   So help me – I will not be made a fool of!

> *First bong of midnight.*

**ALICE**   Yes you will, Karl Pearson. Time makes fools of us all.

> *Blackout. A robust piano version of "Wee Wifey" is heard (à la Beethoven). As for the effect – the cloth is overtop them when the lights come back up, and ALICE pulls it off – so we see the four revealed at the foot of the stage, but they react as they see something revealed to them.*
>
> *The cloth billows. Chimes continue. It is midnight. ALICE steps forward. She finally sees what she has been working towards.*

**ALICE**   That's it. It's cast...

> *There is a pause as the four begin to take in what they are seeing.*

**ADELAIDE**   In Heaven's name...

SILAS      Don't look at it...

KARL      What is this, Alice, this... unnatural...

> *They have stepped onto the silk, looking about themselves. Light swirls around them.*

ALICE      No. It is not unnatural... you made it. From the light and darkness of your own lives. I just... pulled away the handkerchief, so to speak.

> *Her words begin to sink in.*

KARL      Oh my God.

ALICE      And yet it will not remember you. Even though you have created it, the future will not remember your names.

SILAS      For pity's sake...

ADELAIDE      But, how could this possibly...?

AUGUSTA      It's beautiful.

KARL      Alice...

SILAS      No, this cannot be!

ADELAIDE      (*comforting*) Silas...

SILAS      Turn away from it! Avert your eyes!

KARL      (*with rising fear*) Alice... *Alice!*

ALICE      You mustn't be afraid.

> *ALICE looks at all of them.*

Look at it.

> *She moves to the Reverend and places her hand on his shoulder.*

ALICE          What do you see?

               *SILAS opens his eyes and takes in what is before*
               *him. Each will speak evenly in turn...*

SILAS          I was a missionary Baptist minister. Silas Tertius
               Rand. I left the church to live the last half of my life
               at the mercy of God. At the age of forty-five, I
               began a family out of wedlock. I died among the
               Christian Mi'kmaq at the age of eighty. I am buried
               at Hantsport, Nova Scotia. (*freezes*)

ADELAIDE       I was the mother of three– (*including her dead infant*)
               four children and the teacher of thousands.
               Adelaide Hoodless. I was a good woman. But I
               died young. I was fifty-two, my work not finished.
               My home near Brantford, Ontario is a museum
               now. The admission is only one dollar. (*freezes*)

AUGUSTA        I lived to see the Women's College Hospital reopen
               on Gerrard Street in 1902, and I was among the first
               women in Canada to vote, in 1912. I died at the age
               of eighty-six, an Officer of the Order of the British
               Empire. Augusta Stowe-Gullen. While I lived, I
               loved. (*as if she's only just realised it*) And I was
               happy. (*freezes*)

KARL           ...I lived in... I was... I am the father of... (*breaking*
               *down*) Jesus Christ. This is not it. This is not it!
               (*shouting*) This is not what I fucking well meant!
               This is not what I–

               *ALICE touches him and he becomes immediately*
               *calm and resigned.*

               –died in 1936, in England. My work was used
               in Canada and the United States in human
               sterilization programmes. My theories became the
               practices of Adolph Hitler's Nazi Party during
               World War II. I am in any place where people are
               systematically killed to make a country pure. Karl
               Pearson. Karl Pearson. I am the father of racial
               cleansing. (*freezes*)

> *ALICE regards them. The clock continues to*
> *chime. Strains of "Auld Lang Syne" are heard.*

**ALICE**    (*to audience*) To think... our pictures of them look old and dead. And they were once as alive as we are now, cold in this winter air, our hearts still beating, our senses taking everything in. We go home to our loved ones now, we'll hold them in bed, and think of what lies in front of us, all of our triumphs, our defeats. But all there is, is the scent of our beloved's hair on the pillow. Everything else is imaginary. Everything else is yet to be decided. (*deep breath*) Can you smell the alders up on McCaul Street? The snow? Can you hear the bells tolling in the tower at City Hall? It's midnight. The future is still coming.

> *The stage darkens.*

## BUILDING JERUSALEM – AN AFTERWORD

The creation of the text of *Building Jerusalem* came out of a unique and lengthy process of collaboration, research, and ferment. It's not unusual for a writer to either create something from the ground up, or to write-to-order. What is more unusual is to come to a work of art already in progress and be invited to bring yourself fully to it.

In effect, this is what Ross Manson proposed to me in the fall of 1996. He had already devised the idea for a play in which four historical characters greet the New Year at a party hosted by a young girl, rather than the famed society member who'd invited them. Ross had been passed a book entitled *Cassell's Book of In-Door Amusements, Card Games & Fireside Fun*—a Victorian catalogue of parlour games (which furnished the original title of the play)— which offered a leaping-off point both for the plot as well as the style of the play. A fifteen minute version of the piece had been performed at the Tarragon Spring Arts Fair that previous spring, with text written by Ross and Linda Griffiths. It featured music, dancing, game-playing, and the same five characters that are in the finished version of the play. Over a coffee at Bar Italia, Ross told me that those elements were fixed. The rest I could make hay with. We were in agreement that the play would be about confronting the new century. And with this, and a box of research, I began to write scenes.

We were especially interested in investigating the phenomenon of how the present is built by those whose names are lost. But the process of writing in the voices of real people (especially those whose histories may be not well documented) is one fraught with both a real and an exaggerated sense of responsibility. On the one hand, there's no fear of being sued by anyone. On the other, what is the point of using historical figures if you cannot stand behind the portrait you're making? Inevitably, the writing of the characters Augusta Stowe-Gullen, Karl Pearson, Adelaide Hoodless, and Silas Rand became a complicated massing of research, writing, personal ideology, and not least of all, the performance styles and personal leanings of the actors who were playing these characters. So how close are these characterisations to the people they are based on? I know I'm comfortable thinking of them as good metaphors for the time and place they lived in. I tend to think that Silas and Augusta would probably not dislike the interpretations of their personae, probably because as a group, we could identify with them and our own time holds their values in esteem (although we probably would conclude that Silas' zeal was over the top). Adelaide might grudgingly accept the portrait of herself, with perhaps a strong cavil about an apparent tendency to flibbertigibbettness. As for Karl Pearson, I don't think I'd want to be in the room when he saw the play. We all found Pearson's values abhorrent, but I think a certain selectiveness in how he is interpreted in *Building Jerusalem* led us to the conclusions we made about him. At the very least, in the late nineteenth century, Pearson would not have stood out the way he does to us now, and he'd probably want that acknowledged. (There might also be a lecture on the actual uses of statistics in the offing.)

The writing and revising of *Building Jerusalem* took the better part of four years. The draft that was performed was the eleventh, and before that point, three earlier drafts were performed in their entirety. An exhilarating process of performance, workshopping, discussion, and revision saw the play from draft to draft, and at each stage, the text was dissected, restructured, and defended. Ross often took the play away and tinkered with structure and text, making cuts, additions or re-arrangements, and returning it to me to retinker if I wished. Our unspoken agreement was that the play was a fluid thing, and that neither of us would prevent the other from bringing something new to it, or challenging something established. It was through an amazing process of symbiosis and collaboration that my role as a writer was never compromised; in fact, it was preserved to the degree that every time I went back to the play, I had the creative freedom and drive to continue working on it as if I were the only person I had to please with it.

We worked with many people in the creation of this play. Ross Manson, Claudia Moore and Bill Brennan (who performed the music) were the only constants (although after I arrived, the intellectually ferocious Kim Renders became one as well). Silas Rand was played by Bill Coleman, Stephan Beckon, and Martin Julien. Alice by both Sarah Chase (who originated the character and performed it in the play's final form) and Waneta Storms. It was always a challenge to remain true to what someone else had been doing with a character when someone new came into the role, as much as it was to keep growing over the years with the same actor in a role.

There was also the added interest of writing for performers who did not normally perform text because they came from dance backgrounds. Both choreographer Claudia Moore and dancers Stephan

Beckon and Sarah Chase not only rose to the occasion, but long before we got to the final stages, I simply stopped thinking about going easy on them. In fact, Silas Rand must speak some truly wrenching things in this play, and it was always a revelation to hear them coming out of Stephan's mouth. (And later, a deep pleasure to hear them coming out of Martin Julien's.) So too Claudia, who sometimes professed terror of her monologues, and then completely owned them. As for Sarah—who not only located most of the old songs, but also the original parlour-game book—her character was the easiest to write, being an amalgam of Sarah's own sense of wonder and the places she let me take it.

On the other hand, there were those in the company—Kim, Martin, Waneta, and Ross, namely—who had, let's say, less movement experience. A couple of them were upgraded to Two Left Feet status by the time Claudia got through with them. The most amazing thing of all was to see artists from different backgrounds guiding each other through the bramble of new ways of using their bodies and their minds. The end result was, as Alice might have said, a marvellous cross-pollination.

The discussion around the workshop table was enlivened by the commitment of all these actors, as well as members of the company who were involved in other roles. Stage Manager Erica Heyland, Associate Director Mark Christmann and our dramaturge, Linda Griffiths, were a full share of the emotional and intellectual life of the play. And then there were the heroes. Camilla Holland, Volcano's producer, put in endless (not *seemingly* endless) hours bringing the production to fruition. JP Robichaud's easy-going multitasking as lighting designer and stage manager on tour amazed everyone. And Jenny Sinclair gets the purple heart for resewing costumes all through the night before opening in Halifax after everything was stolen from the company van.

Playwrights rarely have the luxury of time or someone else's inspiration to see them though the agonies of the blank page. But with *Building Jerusalem*, I already had Ross Manson's marvellously flexible idea, and then I had the embarrassment of riches in the form of many workshops staffed by great actors. Joe Orton once said that bad writers borrow and good writers steal, and if this play is no good, it's not for lack of opportunities for theft. *Building Jerusalem* was born in a ferment of good ideas and that was its element all throughout the process of its creation. It is also rooted in the earnest and honest values espoused by the people it represents. Some reviewers wrote that *Building Jerusalem* critiques our modern-day certainties by showing up the now-rejected values of the past. But I also think that it pays tribute to people who, like us, move forward knowing very little of what the future will actually hold. No matter how this play treats Stowe-Gullen, Rand, Hoodless, or Pearson, I came to respect these people because I admired the courage they had in their convictions, and that, to me, is as important as any other reading of this play: we define ourselves and our times by fervently seeking out meaning and purpose. That much has not changed, nor will it.

Michael Redhill
Toronto, 2001

*Photo by Bruce Meyer.*

Michael Redhill is a novelist, poet, and playwright. His most recent poetry is *Light-crossing* (House of Anansi Press, 2001), and his novel, *Martin Sloane,* has just been published by Doubleday Canada. He lives in Toronto with his partner and two sons, and is the managing editor of *Brick, A Literary Journal.*